MISSIONS

God's Heart for the World

9 STUDIES FOR INDIVIDUALS OR GROUPS

LifeGuide®
BIBLE STUDIES

PAUL BORTHWICK

IVP Connect

An imprint of InterVarsity Press
Downers Grove, Illinois

InterVarsity Press
P.O. Box 1400, Downers Grove, IL 60515-1426
ivpress.com
email@ivpress.com

InterVarsity Press® is the book-publishing division of InterVarsity Christian Fellowship/USA®, a movement of students and faculty active on campus at hundreds of universities, colleges and schools of nursing in the United States of America, and a member movement of the International Fellowship of Evangelical Students. For information about local and regional activities, visit intervarsity.org.

LifeGuide® is a registered trademark of InterVarsity Christian Fellowship.

All Scripture quotations, unless otherwise indicated, are taken from the Holy Bible, New International Version®. NIV®. *Copyright* ©1973, 1978, 1984 by International Bible Society. *Used by permission of* Zondervan Publishing House. All rights reserved.

Cover photograph: Dennis Flaherty

ISBN 978-0-8308-3090-9

Printed in the United States of America ∞

P	27	26	25	24	23	22	21	20	19	18	17	16	15	14	13	12
Y	30	29	28	27	26	25	24	23	22	21	20	19	18	17	16	15

Contents

GETTING THE MOST OUT OF *MISSIONS* ———————— 5

1 **God the Seeker**   Genesis 3:1-9 ————— 9

2 **Blessed to Be a Blessing**   Genesis 12:1-9 ————— 12

3 **The Lord Reigns**   Psalm 96 ————— 15

4 **God's Attack on Racism**   Jonah 1—4 ————— 18

5 **Concentric-Circle Outreach**   Acts 1:1-11 ————— 21

6 **Ambassadors for Christ**   2 Corinthians 5:11-21 — 25

7 **The Motivational Example**   Philippians 2:1-11 ————— 29

8 **Eyes on the Prize**   Hebrews 11:1—12:3 ——— 33

9 **Diversity in Heaven**   Revelation 7:9-14 ——— 37

Leader's Notes————————————— 41

Getting the Most Out of *Missions*

Morning services at a local church we visited were excellent in many ways. They offered great programs, led the services with outstanding worship and offered good and relevant Bible teaching. But when my wife, Christie, and I discussed it later, we agreed that something was missing. There was little emphasis on outreach to others and mission to the world.

Our discussion then shifted to bigger questions. We asked, "What motivates evangelism, outreach and world missions involvement? Why would individuals or a fellowship group or church dedicate themselves to outreach? What could drive people to give away resources—like time, money or career—to spreading Christ's love to the world?"

It would seem that resources like satellites, the Internet and jet travel would make people even more ready to reach the world. The concept of the global village has dramatically reduced our perception of the size of the earth, even though the world population now exceeds six billion. But, we concluded, the realities of the global village are not reason enough to mobilize us for evangelism and worldwide outreach. If they were, every Christian would be anxious to be involved around the world. Instead the global village often overwhelms us or numbs us into inactivity.

Then I brought up the inequities in the world. "Shouldn't we be motivated," I argued, "by the world of economic haves and have-nots that we live in?" The vast majority of the global population ("Two-Thirds" or more) live as have-nots, struggling to survive and without choices. The remainder of us live in excess, consuming vast amounts of resources on ourselves—often at the expense of the have-nots. But the needs and inequities of the world often serve only to create guilt or "compassion fatigue." The unequal distribution of wealth in the world is not enough to mobilize us for local or global ministry.

As the discussion progressed, we recalled an article in a Christian magazine in which experts reported that the task of world missions is nearly over. They celebrated reports which indicated that the Christian church moves closer daily to "completing the task" of presenting the message of God's love through Jesus Christ to every ethnic group on earth—to the end of establishing self-sustaining churches in those ethnic groups. Is "completing the task" reason enough to mobilize us for evangelism and world outreach?

I thought our discussion would go on for quite a while longer until Christie offered the most succinct response. She said, "It's simple. We're involved in outreach to reflect the character of God. Missions is God's heart."

This Bible study guide focuses on God's heart for lost people as revealed in the Bible—from Genesis to Revelation. It builds on the conviction that at the foundation of our desire to mobilize ourselves, our groups or our local churches for global outreach stands the "heart" or character of God.

The studies do not focus on the typical missionary texts, like the Great Commission of Matthew 28:18-20. Why? Because in the words of David Howard, former director of the Urbana missionary convention, "The missionary enterprise of the church is not a pyramid built upside down with its point on one isolated text in the New Testament out of which we have built a huge structure known as *missions*. Rather, the missionary enterprise of the church is a great pyramid built right side up with its base running from Genesis 1 to Revelation 22. All of Scripture forms the foundation for the outreach of the gospel to the whole world" (*The Great Commission for Today* [Downers Grove, Ill.: InterVarsity Press, 1976], p. 31).

In the Bible, God reveals
☐ his love for lost people
☐ his passion to bring these people back into fellowship with himself
☐ his desire to use our lives to fulfill that purpose
☐ the reality of the sacrifices involved for all three

Because we believe that as followers of Christ our supreme desire is to live our lives in ways that reflect God's character to the world, each study includes something that all of us are asked to do to reflect God's love practically to the world—starting right where we live.

May these Bible studies help you understand, internalize and then demonstrate God's heart for our world.

Suggestions for Individual Study

1. As you begin each study, pray that God will speak to you through his Word.

2. Read the introduction to the study and respond to the personal reflection question or exercise. This is designed to help you focus on God and on the theme of the study.

3. Each study deals with a particular passage—so that you can delve into the author's meaning in that context. Read and reread the passage to be studied. The questions are written using the language of the New International Version, so you may wish to use that version of the Bible. The New Revised Standard Version is also recommended.

4. This is an inductive Bible study, designed to help you discover for yourself what Scripture is saying. The study includes three types of questions. *Observation* questions ask about the basic facts: who, what, when, where and how. *Interpretation* questions delve into the meaning of the passage. *Application* questions help you discover the implications of the text for growing in Christ. These three keys unlock the treasures of Scripture.

Write your answers to the questions in the spaces provided or in a personal journal. Writing can bring clarity and deeper understanding of yourself and of God's Word.

5. It might be good to have a Bible dictionary handy. Use it to look up any unfamiliar words, names or places.

6. Use the prayer suggestion to guide you in thanking God for what you have learned and to pray about the applications that have come to mind.

7. You may want to go on to the suggestion under "Now or Later," or you may want to use that idea for your next study.

Suggestions for Members of a Group Study

1. Come to the study prepared. Follow the suggestions for individual study mentioned above. You will find that careful preparation will greatly enrich your time spent in group discussion.

2. Be willing to participate in the discussion. The leader of your group will not be lecturing. Instead, he or she will be encouraging the members of the group to discuss what they have learned. The leader will be asking the questions that are found in this guide.

3. Stick to the topic being discussed. Your answers should be based on the verses which are the focus of the discussion and not on outside authorities such as commentaries or speakers. These studies focus on a particular passage of Scripture. Only rarely should you refer to other portions of the Bible. This allows for everyone to participate in in-depth study on equal ground.

4. Be sensitive to the other members of the group. Listen attentively when they describe what they have learned. You may be surprised by their insights! Each question assumes a variety of answers. Many questions do not have "right" answers, particularly questions that aim at meaning or application. Instead the questions push us to explore the passage more thoroughly.

When possible, link what you say to the comments of others. Also, be affirming whenever you can. This will encourage some of the more hesitant members of the group to participate.

5. Be careful not to dominate the discussion. We are sometimes so eager to express our thoughts that we leave too little opportunity for others to respond. By all means participate! But allow others to also.

6. Expect God to teach you through the passage being discussed and through the other members of the group. Pray that you will have an enjoyable and profitable time together, but also that as a result of the study you will find ways that you can take action individually and/or as a group.

7. Remember that anything said in the group is considered confidential and should not be discussed outside the group unless specific permission is given to do so.

8. If you are the group leader, you will find additional suggestions at the back of the guide.

1

God the Seeker

Genesis 3:1-9

Why be involved in missions? Our mission in the world is rooted in the character of God. What we do flows from our understanding of who God is. If this is true, then the key question becomes, Who is this God?

GROUP DISCUSSION. When you think of God, what comes to mind? What adjectives or images would you use to describe God's character?

PERSONAL REFLECTION. When you contemplate your own relationship with God, what aspects of God's character are the most personal or intimate to you?

At this point in the Bible the story of creation has been recounted twice in Genesis 1 and 2. Adam and Eve are living in complete harmony in their relationship with God and with each other in an environment that God himself has declared "very good" (Genesis 1:31). *Read Genesis 3:1-9.*

1. What does the serpent do to undermine the harmony of Adam and Eve's relationship with God (vv. 1-5)?

2. Imagine yourself as Eve. What factors would you have been weighing as you decided whether or not to eat the fruit?

What do you think entered into Adam's decision to eat the fruit?

3. Do you think it was wrong for them to know good and evil (v. 5)? Explain.

4. How does Adam and Eve's action affect their relationship with each other (compare Genesis 2:25 with 3:7)?

5. How does Adam and Eve's action affect their relationship with God (v. 8)?

6. Consider God's actions in verses 8-10. What do these verses reveal about him?

7. In a world of people who are rebelling against God, how might we imitate God's action toward Adam and Eve?

8. What difference does it make in your life to know that God came looking for you—even when you were still a lost sinner?

9. Adam and Eve walked away from God because they listened to lies (or at least half-truths). What lies do you see people believing today which separate them from each other and from God?

---

10. Adam and Eve made the choice to sin, yet God, the sinned-against-one in this case, still came looking for them. What is our responsibility for taking the initiative in going out after others, even those who have intentionally wronged us or sinned against God?

---

11. Imagine that you're talking with a friend who insists, "God could never forgive me after all that I've done." How would you use this passage to introduce that person to God's grace?

Ask God to give you the opportunity today to reach out and be his voice, saying to an alienated person, "God loves you; he's looking for you."

Now or Later

Reflect on a time—either past or present—when something in your life made you want to hide from God. Hear God's voice saying, "Where are you?" and rejoice that he never gives up in his pursuit.

Luke's Gospel focuses on God's pursuit of things lost. In Luke 15, Jesus tells us of the pursuit of the lost coin, the lost sheep and the lost son, all as analogies of the loving God looking for us. Read Luke 19:1-10 and observe Jesus saying, "Where are you?" to Zacchaeus. Celebrate your own found-ness as Zacchaeus did, and memorize Luke 19:10 as your mission.

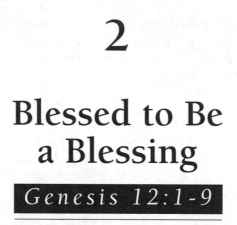

2

Blessed to Be a Blessing

Genesis 12:1-9

After the seeking God finds us and restores us to relationship with him, he sends us out. He calls us to himself so that he can—in biblical language—"bless" us, but he does so for a purpose. God blesses us so that we in turn can bless others. He calls us out of our security and comfort to go out to bless others so that "all nations" can receive his blessing.

GROUP DISCUSSION. When has a move or change been particularly difficult for you?

PERSONAL REFLECTION. Think through your own life. What securities would you have the toughest time leaving behind in order to follow God wherever he wanted to direct you in the world?

Abram (later Abraham) serves as the prototypical missionary. God calls him out from one culture to another and from his comfort zone into a world of faith and dependence on God. God promises to bless him, but he has a specific purpose for this blessing which will affect all nations. *Read Genesis 12:1-9.*

---

1. What commands does the Lord give Abram (12:1)?

2. What promises accompany these commands (12:2-3)?

3. Imagine yourself to be over seventy years old, financially secure with no dependents. Now imagine that God tells you to leave all that security and go to an unknown place. How would you feel?

4. How would you explain the term *blessing* to someone else—especially someone unfamiliar with biblical language?

5. In Genesis 11:4 God judges and condemns the people who intended to build the tower of Babel in an effort to "make a name" for themselves, yet here God promises to make Abram's name great (12:2). What is the difference?

6. It seems that God's call on Abram automatically included Sarai (Sarah), Abram's wife. How does God's call on someone affect their closest relations—friends, family, spouse?

7. After the promises and commands, Abram responds. *Read Genesis 12:6-9.* What characterizes Abram's action?

8. If we are the "children of Abraham," what do these verses tell us about why God blesses us?

9. How has God blessed you (consider resources, family, gifts and abilities, training, experiences, and relationships)?

10. What's a practical step you can take so that God can bless others through you?

11. What action can you take that he might bless other nations through you?

Pause right now and thank God for three or four of the greatest gifts he has given you. Reflect for a few minutes about your greatest fears about the future, then take these fears to God.

Now or Later

Psalm 67 starts with a prayer for God's blessing borrowed from Numbers 6:24-26, but it combines this plea for blessing with an understanding of God's global purposes in blessing his people. You might read this as a prayer for God to use you as he did Abram.

3

The Lord Reigns

Psalm 96

What is the definition of *missions*? Some see images of pith-helmeted, white-skinned people penetrating dark jungles. Others fear that it means a religious version of cultural imperialism. In Psalm 96 the psalmist introduces us to a different definition; he calls us to declare God's glory to all nations. The goal is neither conquest nor human-manipulated conversion. The goal of missions is to see God worshiped.

GROUP DISCUSSION. Imagine that in response to the question "What do you believe?" you said, "The God of Abraham, Isaac and Jacob—who sent Jesus Christ as our Savior—alone is to be worshiped." How do you think people would respond?

PERSONAL REFLECTION. What do you believe about absolute truth? Ask God to shape your convictions through these studies.

The psalmist writes from a context in which diverse deities are worshiped, creating an environment that we call pluralism, in which no one should claim to have the "Truth." Rather than contesting the other religions of that day, the psalmist is engulfed by thoughts about the greatness of God, the central motive for declaring God to the world. *Read Psalm 96.*

---

1. How does the psalmist portray God's character and works in this text?

2. What imperatives call the people of God to action (vv. 1-3)?

What would the actions described here look like in daily living?

3. How does God call us to respond to his holiness and majesty (vv. 4-10)?

4. What does it mean to "proclaim his salvation day after day" (v. 2)?

5. What sets the God of the Bible apart from all other gods (vv. 4-6)?

6. What do you think these verses told the people of the psalmist's time about their response to the pluralistic spirit of their age?

What do these verses tell us regarding our response to the pluralistic spirit of our age that says "Everyone's all right—there's no one right way to God"?

7. God is worshiped by more than just humanity. How does creation declare God's glory?

8. What do verses 7-9 tell us about God's primary goal in missions?

_____

9. What does the text tell us about God's judgment (vv. 9-10, 13)?

How does this affect our motivation or incentive to "declare his glory" to the world?

_____

10. The text refers many times to "all the earth," "the nations," "families of nations" and "the peoples." In what ways does God call you to cross cultural or ethnic boundaries so that you can "declare God's glory among the nations" right where you live?

Pray for two or three people that you have daily contact with who need to hear about God's salvation through you—especially those who worship false gods.

Now or Later

Are there any "false gods" or idols in your own life? Read Psalm 96:5 again and ask God to give you an undivided devotion to him as the one and only true God.

Read Isaiah 49:1-7 with special attention to verse 6. Remember that God is not just concerned about your ethnic group, people or nation. His goal is that his salvation be communicated "to the ends of the earth."

4

God's Attack on Racism

Jonah 1—4

Most people associate Jonah with fear. God called him to preach to the people of Nineveh, his violent and hated neighbors, but Jonah ran the other way. It wasn't Jonah's fear of the Ninevites that made him run. He feared that God might have mercy on people he wanted condemned. Jonah's extreme nationalism (in Jonah's day, each nation was a different race) kept him from wanting to give others a chance to respond to God.

GROUP DISCUSSION. In the news today, what conflicts or civil wars do you see that are based on peoples' long-term hatred of each other? What causes such long-term hostility? How do you think the Christian message of reconciliation could change these circumstances?

PERSONAL REFLECTION. Think of your own ethnic heritage. Are there any people or nations that you have learned to think of in a negative light? Ask God to use the story of Jonah to help you understand his love for all peoples.

We know Jonah because of his rebellion against God and the three-day excursion in the belly of a great fish (although we hear of "Jonah and the whale," the Bible refers only to a great fish [1:17]). Called to Nineveh, Jonah runs (chap. 1), repents in the belly of the fish (chap. 2), obeys God and preaches in Nineveh (chap. 3), and then resents God's mercy (chap. 4). *Read Jonah 1.*

---

1. Tarshish is the opposite direction of Nineveh—where God was calling Jonah. When have you felt tempted to run from God's call to you?

---

2. Contrast Jonah's reaction to the storm with the sailors' reaction.

---

3. How does God use Jonah—even in his rebellion—to direct non-Jews to worship the God of Israel?

---

4. *Read Jonah 2.* From the belly of the fish, Jonah prays. What aspects of God's character become very real to Jonah in this crisis?

---

5. What does Jonah vow to do if God delivers him?

---

6. *Read Jonah 3.* Some think that God "puts us on the shelf" and doesn't use us to serve him if we disobey him. What does Jonah teach us about God's mercy toward his people?

---

7. Describe Jonah's ministry as summarized in 3:1-4.

8. How do the king and the people of Nineveh respond to Jonah (3:5-9)?

---

9. Contrast God's first call (1:2), Jonah's sermon (3:4) and God's response to the people of Nineveh (3:10). What happened?

---

10. *Read Jonah 4.* Chapter 4 begins with Jonah's unhappiness. What do we learn about the real reason Jonah ran in chapter 1?

---

11. What is God's purpose in giving Jonah the experience of the vine, the worm and the wind?

---

12. Think of yourself as Jonah. Who would be the Ninevites in your life?

---

13. What are the implications of the book of Jonah for our call to go across cultures and ethnicities to proclaim the love of God through Jesus Christ to our world?

Is there any person that you're afraid God will call you to love? Pray for God's heart of compassion to help you overcome your fears.

Now or Later

Read John 4:1-26. Compare Jesus' responses to the culturally alienated Samaritan woman with Jonah's outreach to the Ninevites.

5

Concentric-Circle Outreach

Acts 1:1-11

We're all instinctively ethnocentric. We tend to think of our own "people"—culture, language, country and socioeconomic group—as superior to others. But the mission heart of God calls us to rise above ethnocentricity. He empowers us to overcome our pride and fears, and he sends us out as his witnesses locally and crossculturally, even to the "ends of the earth."

GROUP DISCUSSION. When you think of trying to build relationships and sharing the love of Christ across cultures, what fears come to mind?

PERSONAL REFLECTION. In what ways do you sense God's power in your witness for him?

In the book of Acts, Luke (also the author of the Gospel of Luke) continues his explanation of the work of God through the Lord Jesus Christ and the Holy Spirit. In Acts we find Jesus—after his crucifixion, burial and resurrection—convincing his followers of his power over death and preparing them for his departure so that the Holy Spirit can come. *Read Acts 1:1-11.*

1. How do you think the disciples were feeling at this time?

2. Why did Jesus tell them to wait in verse 4?

3. What do these verses tell us about Luke's intent in writing Acts?

4. Verse 3 tells us that Jesus spoke about the kingdom of God. What does the disciples' question in verse 6 tell us about what they were thinking when Jesus referred to the kingdom?

5. Why do you think we are not allowed to know the specifics about the "end times" (v. 7)?

6. What connection (if any) is there between Jesus' postresurrection demonstrations cited in verse 3 and his promise of "power" in verse 8?

7. Paraphrase Acts 1:8 in a way that reflects how those disciples might have heard this command. Now paraphrase the way you understand it.

8. What do verses 9-11 tell us about the way in which Jesus will come to earth a second time?

9. What is the connection between the Holy Spirit's power and our witness in the world?

10. Jerusalem, Judea, Samaria and the ends of the earth describe our concentric circles of outreach, the ever-widening ripples that followers of Jesus Christ are supposed to touch. Think through the applications for your outreach as Christ's witness. Who is your Jerusalem (consider neighbors, roommates, friends, family and work associates)?

Who is your Judea (perhaps people in your town, city, state or province)?

Who is your Samaria (think of those who are geographically close but culturally distant, such as institutionalized people, homeless people and HIV sufferers)?

Who is your "ends of the earth" (other-language speakers, international students and people in other countries you'll pray for or go to serve)?

Pray a concentric-circle prayer today, starting with prayers for the people closest to you and rippling out to diverse people from all over the world.

Now or Later

Think through the reality of the power of God that raised Jesus Christ from the dead. Then reflect on and perhaps journal about how that power might affect your life as a witness for Christ.

Read Acts 8:1-40. In this passage we find that the growing church in Acts 2 didn't follow the command of Acts 1:8. Instead, that church, like many of us, stayed in its own comfort zone until God launched the Christians out into Judea and Samaria through a great persecution. Philip exemplifies a Spirit-empowered witness in this chapter, crossing over cultural barriers to bring the gospel first to the Samaritans and then to Africa through the Ethiopian.

6

Ambassadors
for Christ

In this passage Paul describes our motive for witness in the world by remembering the work that Christ has done and the ministry that he has given us. We now serve as Christ's ambassadors. The Corinthian readers, many of whom were slaves or impoverished, had to go through a paradigm shift to think of themselves as ambassadors. From their perspective an ambassador spoke on behalf of the Roman emperor, delivering his message to the people. An ambassador therefore carried great authority and great responsibility.

God could have communicated his love to the world through any means he desired. For reasons that are unfathomable to us, he chooses to do his work through us. We are his method. We serve as his ambassadors communicating the message of reconciliation through Jesus Christ to the world.

GROUP DISCUSSION. What images from daily life, history or the Bible does the word *reconciliation* bring to mind?

PERSONAL REFLECTION. Who served as "Christ's ambassador" to you, telling you the good news that God wanted a restored relationship with you through Jesus Christ? Spend a few minutes thanking God for that person. Paul wrote to the Corinthians to teach them about their newfound faith and to serve as an example to them—to the point that he tells them to "follow my example as I follow the example of Christ" (1 Corinthians 11:1). In this passage he exemplifies the motive and method for carrying Christ's message to the world. *Read 2 Corinthians 5:11-21.*

---

1. What were Paul's motives for ministry (vv. 11, 14, 21)?

How do such diverse motives fit together?

---

2. In specific ways, how might a person's life look when he or she is living according to Paul's description in 5:15?

---

3. What does it mean to regard others "from a worldly point of view" (v. 16)?

4. How does this passage (especially v. 21) describe the reconciliation that God has provided for us?

---

5. How do our reconciliation to God (v. 18) and our transformation in Christ (v. 17) relate to our outward ministry (vv. 18-20)?

---

6. Consider your daily life. How does being reconciled to God (v. 21) relate to the ministry of reconciliation (v. 18) and the message of reconciliation (v. 19)?

---

7. What do you see as your role and your responsibility as an "ambassador" for Christ?

---

8. How can the combined motives of the fear of God and the love of Christ affect your incentive for sharing Christ with others?

9. If God "makes his appeal" for reconciliation with others through us (v. 20), what responsibility do we have for the conversion of others?

---

10. What will it mean for you to enter the next week with a transformed self-image (v. 17), living as one becoming "the righteousness of God" (v. 21), especially as it pertains to seeing yourself as Christ's "ambassador" (v. 20) to your world?

Invite God to show you a new opportunity to be his ambassador in the year ahead.

Now or Later

Read Isaiah 6:1-8 as an example of God reconciling someone (Isaiah) by confronting that person with

☐ God's awesome character (the "fear" of the Lord)

☐ the person's own sin (therefore the need for reconciliation)

☐ God's solution (to forgive sin)

☐ God's inquiry (who will go?)

☐ the person's willingness to serve as God's ambassador ("Here am I; send me")

7

The Motivational Example

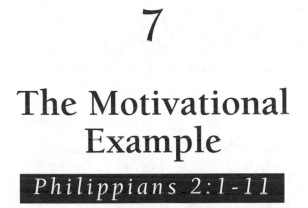

Philippians 2:1-11

Our culture tells us to respond to a challenge with the comeback "What's in this for me?" Yet outreach, missions and service involve communicating God's love to our world in ways that will inevitably involve our loss of comfort and sacrifice of our personal rights. Where do we find the sustained motivation for such giving?

GROUP DISCUSSION. When you think of self-sacrifice and selfless service to others, who comes to mind? Describe that person. What characterizes his or her life? Where do we find the sustained motivation for such giving?

PERSONAL REFLECTION. In thinking about your service to others, either in your own culture or somewhere else in the world, what potential losses do you fear most?

Paul wrote the book of Philippians while in some sort of captivity, either prison or, more likely, a type of house arrest that had him chained to a Roman soldier twenty-four hours a day. From this context he wrote the letter to the church at Philippi, which we have in four chapters. The letter is characterized by the word *joy*, which provokes readers to ask, "How could Paul find joy in the midst of such difficult circumstances?" *Read Philippians 2:1-11.*

---

1. What do verses 1-5 reveal about Paul's purpose in setting Jesus forth as our example? (Read Philippians 4:2-3 as well.)

---

2. How would you feel about receiving a letter like this?

---

3. Describe the progression downward and upward of Jesus' service (vv. 6-8) and then reward (vv. 9-11).

---

4. What did Jesus need to release in order to come to earth to serve humanity (vv. 6-8)?

Why did Jesus release all this—even allowing himself to be taken to the point of death on a cross?

---

5. No matter what the challenges described in this passage—servant-hood, humanity, humility and even death—it seems that Jesus entered these sacrifices by choice: he "made himself nothing" (v. 7). How does this passage apply to times when we choose suffering?

In what ways would you apply this passage to those living under hardships they didn't choose (like Paul's house arrest)?

_____

6. Notice in verses 6-8 that Jesus had to come into the world in order to reach lost humanity; he couldn't reach them in the same way from heaven (vv. 6-7). What "worlds" might you need to go into so that others can know the love of God?

_____

7. In this passage, Paul writes of Jesus' incarnation (vv. 6-8) and his glorification (vv. 9-11). Imagine that you are imprisoned with Paul for preaching the gospel. How might these realities serve to motivate you to endure prison hardships and to continue serving others?

_____

8. How do you think the phrase "made himself nothing" (v. 7) applies to our serving others?

_____

9. What does this passage teach us about God's perspective on sacrifice in this life and rewards in the next (vv. 9-11)?

_____

10. What role do you think the heavenly reward (vv. 9-11) played in Jesus' obedience in service and sacrifice?

What role should the prospect of eternal or heavenly reward play in motivating us toward sacrificial service?

_____

11. Imagine that you're contemplating a crosscultural service project to work with extremely poor people. You're recruiting others to support you financially, and someone asks, "Do you mean that you're actually paying to go and work in these squalid conditions?" How might you use this passage as your basis for responding?

Ask God to lead you into a specific "world" this week—even at risk or cost to yourself—so that someone else might experience the love of Jesus through you.

Now or Later
To continue the study of the motivational example of Jesus, *read 1 John 3:16-20.* How does John exhort his readers to follow the example of Jesus (v. 16)?

What form does this "laying down our lives" take in practical daily living (v. 17)?

What are the characteristics of the love that God wants us to express (v. 18)?

What effect on our consciences does God promise when we act out his love in this way (vv. 19-20)?

8

Eyes on
the Prize

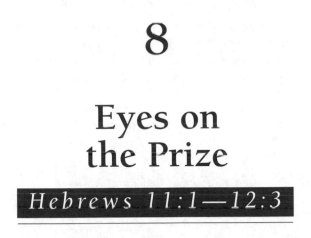

Hebrews 11:1—12:3

It does not take much research into world missions, either present or past, to find the ground littered with casualties. It's tough to follow Jesus, and if we enter into the spiritual battle of taking the good news of Jesus where no one has heard of him, the battle will intensify. How can we find the stamina to keep on going and not quit? This was the exact issue facing the people who received this book of Hebrews.

GROUP DISCUSSION. Discuss your heroes of the faith, either people of biblical times or others from Christian history (you can even cite people who are alive today). Why do you consider them heroes? What is it about their faith that you'd like to emulate? Is there anything about their lives that you'd rather not imitate?

PERSONAL REFLECTION. When was the last time you really stepped out in faith into a place which took you out of your own comfort zone, into a place where you had to trust God? As you prepare for this study, ask God to awaken your faith and help you go beyond where you are now.

The readers of the book of Hebrews were discouraged. Persecution and hardship caused many of them to consider abandoning their faith. To encourage their endurance, the writer of Hebrews presents them with a rundown of the great Old Testament saints who went before them and then concludes with Jesus, all toward the goal of helping them stay "in the race" and not quit. *Read Hebrews 11:1—12:3.*

1. According to Hebrews 11:1, what is the biblical definition of faith?

What does this mean?

2. In the entire chapter, who is your favorite character (other than Jesus)? How or why do you relate to him or her?

3. Based on what you know about some of these characters (Abraham, Moses, David, Samson), what would you say to the person who says that God uses only perfect people who "have it all together"?

4. As you face your own future and even contemplate the possibility of crosscultural service in another place, how might you draw strength from Abraham's story (11:8-9)?

5. What long-term vision did these people of faith share, even Jesus (11:6, 10, 13-16, 25-26; 12:2)?

How does this vision inspire you?

6. Some teach that following Jesus guarantees success, wealth and health. How does this compare with the faith accounts of 11:32-38?

7. How does this passage encourage you to have a bolder faith?

In what ways are these examples frightening to you?

8. Imagine that you're writing a letter to coworkers who are serving in a very difficult place (surrounded by violence or poverty or religious opposition) where it would be easy to lose heart and quit the faith. How would you use this passage to encourage them?

9. How can you apply the command to "fix your eyes on Jesus" in the week ahead?

10. What steps of faith and what types of sacrifices might we be willing to make if our eyes are on the "joy set before us"?

Ask God for an opportunity to step out in faith this week, and then ask for the courage to take the opportunity when it comes.

Now or Later

Read Philippians 3:7-14. Keeping the eyes-on-the-prize runner's worldview in mind, notice how Paul describes his passion to know Christ, the power of his resurrection and the fellowship of sharing in his sufferings. How does Paul's passion affect the way he looks at past accomplishments?

What does the passion to know Christ do to Paul's sense of focus and purpose?

What causes Paul to "strain ahead" to finish the race?

9

Diversity in Heaven

Revelation 7:9-14

Do you ever wonder how heaven looks? If a "heavenly vision" (see Revelation 8) is supposed to motivate us to endure and tolerate hardship, what does this vision look like? Are we all playing harps and using our wings to float from cloud to cloud? Is it just a world-without-end choir concert?

The book of Revelation (a.k.a. the Apocalypse) gives us the clearest vision of heaven, even though it's filled with symbols. Several of the clearest heavenly visions tell us that the work of missions has been accomplished, and the great multicultural family of God has come together to celebrate.

GROUP DISCUSSION. What in the Bible's teaching on heaven do you understand such that you can say, "This we know for sure about heaven"?

PERSONAL REFLECTION. Jonah's racism (Jonah 4) prevented him from wanting any Ninevites in heaven. Do you have any such biases? If so, ask God to prepare you for the challenge of the text ahead.

Revelation has had many interpretations over the nineteen hundred or more years since John first wrote these words. Some say the entire book of prophecy was fulfilled in the first century. Others believe it's futuristic only, targeting the specific events just preceding the end of the world. Still others believe that it represents epochs or eras of Christian history. The only thing that most agree on is that it is a depiction of God's final victory over evil in human history. Among the testimonies of this victory are the glorious heavenly worship services that John experiences. Our text takes us to one of these worship events. *Read Revelation 7:9-14.*

---

1. Describe the crowd that John sees.

---

2. Why does the writer emphasize that people from every nation, tribe, people and language are present?

---

3. What would it have felt like to be a part of this crowd?

---

4. Think about worship experiences you have had with people from backgrounds different from yours. What was that like?

5. What is their worship song?

---

6. Who is the Lamb (read also Revelation 5:8-10)?

---

7. What are the worshipers wearing, and what do you think this attire symbolizes (v. 14)?

---

8. What have these worshipers endured (vv. 13-14)?

---

9. Analyze the words of the saints' worship as well as the angels'. How much focus is on *who* God is, and how much on *what* God has done for us?

How does this compare with the worship style in your church?

10. How do these verses encourage you to endure whatever tribulations and hardships you might be facing?

---

11. What does this passage (especially 7:9) say to the church of Jesus Christ today in light of facts like (1) there are over a billion people who have never heard of Jesus Christ, (2) there are still several thousand languages with no written translation of the Bible, and (3) whole ethnic groups (what John calls "peoples" or "tribes") still have no witnessing church?

Thank God for creating a world of people who love him.

Now or Later

Read Acts 10. This passage shows the struggle of Peter and the early church to accept the reality of a multicultural body of Christ. Read it through noticing the struggle that both parties faced in accepting each other as equals. Take note of the ways that God brought people together through both the miraculous (visions) and the pragmatic (an in-home visit, a meal together and so on).

Look for an opportunity in the next month to worship at a church that is ethnically different from your own. Go participate in a worship service with the prayer, "Lord, give me a taste of heaven today."

Leader's Notes

MY GRACE IS SUFFICIENT FOR YOU. (2 COR 12:9)

Leading a Bible discussion can be an enjoyable and rewarding experience. But it can also be *scary*—especially if you've never done it before. If this is your feeling, you're in good company. When God asked Moses to lead the Israelites out of Egypt, he replied, "O Lord, please send someone else to do it"! (Ex 4:13). It was the same with Solomon, Jeremiah and Timothy, but God helped these people in spite of their weaknesses, and he will help you as well.

You don't need to be an expert on the Bible or a trained teacher to lead a Bible discussion. The idea behind these inductive studies is that the leader guides group members to discover for themselves what the Bible has to say. This method of learning will allow group members to remember much more of what is said than a lecture would.

These studies are designed to be led easily. As a matter of fact, the flow of questions through the passage from observation to interpretation to application is so natural that you may feel that the studies lead themselves. This study guide is also flexible. You can use it with a variety of groups—student, professional, neighborhood or church groups. Each study takes forty-five to sixty minutes in a group setting.

There are some important facts to know about group dynamics and encouraging discussion. The suggestions listed below should enable you to effectively and enjoyably fulfill your role as leader.

Preparing for the Study

1. Ask God to help you understand and apply the passage in your own life. Unless this happens, you will not be prepared to lead others. Pray too for the various members of the group. Ask God to open your hearts to the message of his Word and motivate you to action.

2. Read the introduction to the entire guide to get an overview of the entire book and the issues which will be explored.

3. As you begin each study, read and reread the assigned Bible passage to familiarize yourself with it.

4. This study guide is based on the New International Version of the Bible. It will help you and the group if you use this translation as the basis for your study and discussion.

5. Carefully work through each question in the study. Spend time in meditation and reflection as you consider how to respond.

6. Write your thoughts and responses in the space provided in the study guide. This will help you to express your understanding of the passage clearly.

7. It might help to have a Bible dictionary handy. Use it to look up any unfamiliar words, names or places. (For additional help on how to study a passage, see chapter five of *How to Lead a LifeGuide Bible Study,* InterVarsity Press.)

8. Consider how you can apply the Scripture to your life. Remember that the group will follow your lead in responding to the studies. They will not go any deeper than you do.

9. Once you have finished your own study of the passage, familiarize yourself with the leader's notes for the study you are leading. These are designed to help you in several ways. First, they tell you the purpose the study guide author had in mind when writing the study. Take time to think through how the study questions work together to accomplish that purpose. Second, the notes provide you with additional background information or suggestions on group dynamics for various questions. This information can be useful when people have difficulty understanding or answering a question. Third, the leader's notes can alert you to potential problems you may encounter during the study.

10. If you wish to remind yourself of anything mentioned in the leader's notes, make a note to yourself below that question in the study.

Leading the Study

1. Begin the study on time. Open with prayer, asking God to help the group to understand and apply the passage.

2. Be sure that everyone in your group has a study guide. Encourage the group to prepare beforehand for each discussion by reading the introduction to the guide and by working through the questions in the study.

3. At the beginning of your first time together, explain that these studies are meant to be discussions, not lectures. Encourage the members of the group to participate. However, do not put pressure on those who may be hesitant to speak during the first few sessions. You may want to suggest the following guidelines to your group.

☐ Stick to the topic being discussed.

☐ Your responses should be based on the verses which are the focus of the discussion and not on outside authorities such as commentaries or speakers.

☐ These studies focus on a particular passage of Scripture. Only rarely should you refer to other portions of the Bible. This allows for everyone to participate in in-depth study on equal ground.

☐ Anything said in the group is considered confidential and will not be discussed outside the group unless specific permission is given to do so.

☐ We will listen attentively to each other and provide time for each person present to talk.

☐ We will pray for each other.

4. Have a group member read the introduction at the beginning of the discussion.

5. Every session begins with a group discussion question. The question or activity is meant to be used before the passage is read. The question introduces the theme of the study and encourages group members to begin to open up. Encourage as many members as possible to participate, and be ready to get the discussion going with your own response.

This section is designed to reveal where our thoughts or feelings need to be transformed by Scripture. That is why it is especially important not to read the passage before the discussion question is asked. The passage will tend to color the honest reactions people would otherwise give because they are, of course, supposed to think the way the Bible does.

You may want to supplement the group discussion question with an icebreaker to help people to get comfortable. See the community section of *Small Group Idea Book* for more ideas.

You also might want to use the personal reflection question with your group. Either allow a time of silence for people to respond individually or discuss it together.

6. Have a group member (or members if the passage is long) read aloud the passage to be studied. Then give people several minutes to read the passage again silently so that they can take it all in.

7. Question 1 will generally be an overview question designed to briefly survey the passage. Encourage the group to look at the whole passage, but try to avoid getting sidetracked by questions or issues that will be addressed later in the study.

8. As you ask the questions, keep in mind that they are designed to be used just as they are written. You may simply read them aloud. Or you may prefer to express them in your own words.

There may be times when it is appropriate to deviate from the study guide. For example, a question may have already been answered. If so, move on to the next question. Or someone may raise an important question not covered in the guide. Take time to discuss it, but try to keep the group from going off on tangents.

9. Avoid answering your own questions. If necessary, repeat or rephrase them until they are clearly understood. Or point out something you read in the leader's notes to clarify the context or meaning. An eager group quickly becomes passive and silent if they think the leader will do most of the talking.

10. Don't be afraid of silence. People may need time to think about the question before formulating their answers.

11. Don't be content with just one answer. Ask, "What do the rest of you think?" or "Anything else?" until several people have given answers to the question.

12. Acknowledge all contributions. Try to be affirming whenever possible. Never reject an answer. If it is clearly off-base, ask, "Which verse led you to that conclusion?" or again, "What do the rest of you think?"

13. Don't expect every answer to be addressed to you, even though this will probably happen at first. As group members become more at ease, they will begin to truly interact with each other. This is one sign of healthy discussion.

14. Don't be afraid of controversy. It can be very stimulating. If you don't resolve an issue completely, don't be frustrated. Move on and keep it in mind for later. A subsequent study may solve the problem.

15. Periodically summarize what the group has said about the passage. This helps to draw together the various ideas mentioned and gives continuity to the study. But don't preach.

16. At the end of the Bible discussion you may want to allow group members a time of quiet to work on an idea under "Now or Later." Then discuss what you experienced. Or you may want to encourage group members to work on these ideas between meetings. Give an opportunity during the session for people to talk about what they are learning.

17. Conclude your time together with conversational prayer, adapting the prayer suggestion at the end of the study to your group. Ask for God's help in following through on the commitments you've made.

18. End on time.

Many more suggestions and helps are found in *How to Lead a LifeGuide Bible Study.*

Components of Small Groups

A healthy small group should do more than study the Bible. There are four components to consider as you structure your time together.

Nurture. Small groups help us to grow in our knowledge and love of God. Bible study is the key to making this happen and is the foundation of your small group.

Community. Small groups are a great place to develop deep friendships with other Christians. Allow time for informal interaction before and after each study. Plan activities and games that will help you get to know each other. Spend time having fun together—going on a picnic or cooking dinner together.

Worship and prayer. Your study will be enhanced by spending time praising God together in prayer or song. Pray for each other's needs—and keep track of how God is answering prayer in your group. Ask God to help you to apply what you are learning in your study.

Outreach. Reaching out to others can be a practical way of applying what you are learning, and it will keep your group from becoming self-focused. Host a series of evangelistic discussions for your friends or neighbors. Clean up the yard of an elderly friend. Serve at a soup kitchen together, or spend a day working on a Habitat house.

Many more suggestions and helps in each of these areas are found in *Small Group Idea Book.* Information on building a small group can be found in *Small Group Leaders' Handbook* and *The Big Book on Small Groups* (both from InterVarsity Press). Reading through one of these books would be worth your time.

Study 1. God the Seeker. Genesis 3:1-9.

Purpose: To show that our outreach to others is based on God's loving character. We follow his example into a lost world, and we say, as his representatives, "Where are you? God wants you back."

General note. This passage records the biblical account of the Fall, when human beings decided to listen to the lies of the deceiver rather than obey the mandates of their loving God.

For the purposes of understanding our mission in the world—namely, imitating God's initiative toward lost people—we stick with just the first nine verses, although you're wise to read on so that you're not deterred by questions related to the consequences of the Fall (Gen 3:10).

Question 1. We learn from other passages of Scripture that the serpent is the deceiver (2 Cor 11:2), also called the devil and Satan (Rev 12:9). As the "father of lies" (Jn 8:44) he undermines the harmony of Adam and Eve's relationship with God by questioning whether they heard God right: "Did God really say?" (v. 1). He entices them to "be like God" (3:4) and promises that they won't die. He sets God up as the jealous and insecure one, telling Adam and Eve that God simply doesn't want them to know what he knows.

Why didn't Adam and Eve die after they ate the forbidden fruit? Although they did not drop dead immediately, sin entered the world through their disobedience, and so as a consequence did death (1 Cor 15:21-22).

Question 2. Many draw a parallel between the threefold attractiveness of the fruit and John's description of the temptations of "the world" in 1 John 2:15-17. In this case, "good for food" parallels "the cravings of sinful man"; "pleasing to the eye" parallels "the lust of his eyes"; "desirable for gaining wisdom" parallels "the boasting of what he has" ("pride of life" in some translations).

Was it wrong for them to desire to know good and evil (Gen 3:5)? In keeping with other passages which urge us to gain wisdom and flee from evil, we must conclude that their sin was simply that of disobedience. God knew that their pure and innocent fellowship in a sin-free environment would be destroyed forever by their rebellion. God had commanded them to abstain from that tree because he had a view of the long-term ramifications of their action.

Questions 3-4. The Bible teaches that when sin entered the world through Adam and Eve's rebellion, multiple relationships were severed: (1) our relationship with God—sin causes a great rift between us and God (Is 59:2), and we come under the curse of death (Gen 3:19; Rom 6:23); (2) our relationship with each other, symbolized by Adam and Eve's sudden awareness of nakedness as well as their tendency to start blaming each other (Gen 3:11-12); (3) our relationship with nature, indicated by the curse on the soil with pain, thorns and thistles (Gen 3:17-18) in place of what must have been pre-Fall ease (Gen 2:28-30).

Question 5. The Bible does indeed teach God's omniscience, omnipotence and omnipresence. Therefore, God knew where Adam and Eve were hiding. His question in Genesis 3:9 is obviously uttered for Adam and Eve's sake (and ours!). He knew where they were, but he wanted them to know that in spite of their sin he was now looking for them.

The question previews the grace of God expressed through Jesus Christ— that while we were still sinners (in hiding) Christ died for us (Rom 5:8). God came looking for Adam and Eve in the garden. God came looking for us in Jesus Christ.

You might draw from the action of God in grace toward Adam and Eve in verse 21. Without stretching the analogy, it's obvious that in order to create garments of skin to cover their nakedness, an animal had to die—to cover the effect of their sin. In the same way, God sent Jesus as the Lamb of God to die—to cover the effects of our sins (Is 53:6).

Question 6. God exemplifies initiative-taking love. God knew where they were, what they had done and why they had done it; nevertheless, he still came looking.

Question 7. We go out into the world because we're following his example to go out in search of those who are lost—regardless of how they got there.

Here you might add to the study by taking five to ten minutes for people to thumb through some popular magazines and tear out commercials (or even articles) which build on lies designed to entice us toward something that promises to make us wiser, better looking, richer or more self-sufficient.

Question 8. It might be useful either to share your own testimony at this juncture or to ask another group member (in advance) to share his or hers.

Question 9. This question might provoke some intense discussion, especially from people who have been sinned against by abusive parents or a painful past. Try to direct the conversation toward the awesomeness of God's initiative toward us. The following biblical stories illustrate God's grace stimulating people to imitate his outgoing, forgiving spirit toward others: (1) Joseph forgiving his brothers for selling him into slavery (Gen 45:4-11 and 50:15-21); (2) Stephen, while being stoned to death, imitating Jesus by asking that God forgive his murderers (Acts 7:60); (3) Paul and Silas, reaching out with care to the jailer who held them in captivity (Acts 16:22-30).

Familiarizing yourself with the great missionary story of Elisabeth Elliot and Rachel Saint's return to work with the Auca (now called Waorani) Indians in Ecuador might be useful as you discuss this question. In January 1956, Elisabeth's husband, Jim, and Rachel's brother, Nate, were part of a group of five killed by the Auca warriors. A year later Rachel and Elisabeth (with Elisabeth's two-year-old daughter, Valerie) returned to the Aucas to be God's visible "Where are you?" to these people. (Elisabeth's books *Through Gates of Splendor* and *The Savage My Kinsman* describe this great story.)

Question 10. "Is there a sin that God cannot forgive?" arises often from the inquiring minds of new Christians. In reassuring group members of God's grace, keep two truths in balance: (1) The only sin Jesus calls "unforgivable" is the sin against or blasphemy of the Holy Spirit (Mt 12:31), which is the complete and lifelong rejection of the saving power and love of Jesus Christ. (2) When God forgives us, he removes our sins "as far as the east is from the west" (Ps 103:12). Through Jesus Christ he grants us forgiveness and a fresh start. It is the overwhelming gratitude of being forgiven that motivates us to go out and declare his forgiveness to others. (3) But we should never take sin lightly or take forgiveness for granted. Remember that although Adam and Eve were pursued and forgiven by God, they still lived out the consequences of their sins (Gen 3:16-19).

Now or Later. These sections after each study can be handled as an extension of your small group if time allows, or you can encourage group members to complete these sections between studies.

In this first study, "Now or Later" focuses on Jesus' New Testament mission in seeking lost things. In the three parables of Luke 15 (lost coin, lost son, lost sheep), Jesus depicts God as the active seeker. Then Jesus illustrates this through his own life by seeking after Zacchaeus in Luke 19:1-10. Zacchaeus had perhaps already heard that this Jesus was the "friend" of tax collectors (Lk 7:34), so he wanted to meet this man. Perhaps Zacchaeus felt condemned by all of the other religious leaders of the day, but Jesus was different and welcomed sinners. See Luke 18:9-14 as an example of the Pharisee's attitude toward tax collectors. The story speaks for itself, with Luke 19:10 being the culmination of God's seeking heart manifested in Jesus.

This continuation study might provoke some good discussion on how we refer to the spiritual state of those outside of Christ. In our age of political correctness, we call people "seekers" or say they are "on the spiritual journey." Jesus called them "lost."

Study 2. Blessed to Be a Blessing. Genesis 12:1-9.

Purpose: To show that the sending God calls us, sends us, blesses us and gives promises to his people so that others across the world can receive God's blessings through us.

General note. This is one of several promises concerning Abram's (later Abraham [Gen 17:5]) fatherhood of the people of God and God's desire to bless the nations on earth through Abram and his line. To illustrate God's relationship with Abram throughout this study, you're wise to read the other parallel passages (Gen 13:14-17; 15:1-5; 17:1-8; 18:18-19; 22:15-18) to observe the contrasts and comparisons of the promises.

Question 1. Stephen's report on this account (recorded as his sermon to the religious leaders in Acts 7:2-53) indicates that the promise was given in Ur and was reiterated in Haran (Gen 12:4) after his father died (Acts 7:4). "The land I will show you" would be Canaan, the Promised Land.

The command to leave his father's household was a much greater challenge for Abram and Sarai than it would be for us today. It meant leaving security and a guaranteed future. It also meant leaving behind the family gods (Josh 24:2 indicates that Terah worshiped heathen gods) and following God alone.

Question 2. God promises Abram blessings in various forms. He promises a great nation—which meant both land and people (the people of Israel as well as those of us who are children of Abraham by faith (as in Rom 4:16-17). He also promised a great name, which referred to both fame and heirs. The third part of the promise includes protection—to the extent that cursing Abram equaled cursing God. Finally, God promised him a global impact.

Question 4. What is a "blessing"? Generally speaking, it's something good or desirable. In this passage we see it manifested in material prosperity (Gen 13:2; 24:35), God's presence (Gen 21:22), admiration from the world (Gen 23:6) and friendship with God (Is 41:8).

Hebrews 11 adds to our understanding here in that it clarifies that by faith Abraham was looking to the eternal fulfillment of these promises—to the eternal inheritance (Heb 11:10, 13-16).

Question 5. The architects of the Tower of Babel (Gen 11:1-9) designed the tower to make their own names great, perhaps with the same spirit expressed by Lucifer in Isaiah 14:12-14. What's the difference with Abram? In Abram's case it was God who would make Abram's name great for the sake of God's glory and for the sake of spreading God's blessings to the nations.

Question 6. It's okay to leave this as an open discussion item. There's no need to reach a conclusive ending. The only thing you should note is the contrast between our times (when spouses desire egalitarian relationships) and Abram and Sarai's time, when a woman had neither the education nor expectation of a modern woman. For Sarai, her husband was her "master" (1 Pet 3:6); she expected him to hear God's voice for the sake of the whole family. The same was true with children: the father was the "patriarch," who was to be obeyed (observe Isaac's compliance as his father tied him to the altar in Gen 22).

Today it's vital that husbands and wives (and engaged couples) hear God's voice together. If one is planning a life of missions and the other is planning a life of materialism, something needs to get resolved before the relationship can move ahead.

Question 7. Abraham exemplifies obedience: "So Abram left, as the LORD had told him" (12:4). Lot goes with Abram (12:4-5), possibly to provide an heir to Abram's possessions.

Note though that there may have been delays between the time when the first call came in Ur, the time when the clan of Terah moved to Haran (Gen 11:31), the time when Abram's father died (Gen 11:32 and Acts 7:3-4) and the time when Abram left (Gen 12:4). Abram's departure illustrates faith (Heb 11:8), but there was also an element of God's patience with him as time probably passed between the first call and the actual departure.

God promises to bless all nations through Abram. God is not intent on Abram's physical heirs only; such nationalism is "too small a thing" for God (see Is 49:6). Instead God desires to bless "all peoples on earth" (Gen 12:3) or "all nations on earth" (Gen 22:18) through Abram.

The point to underscore here is that God blesses us so that we in turn can bless others. Abram became the father of all of the Hebrew and Arab world through his sons, Isaac and Ishmael. Even greater than that, however, Abram blessed all the nations by becoming the father of those who are justified by faith (compare Gen 15:6; Rom 4; Gal 3:10-14).

Question 8. By faith we are Abram's children (Rom 4). If this is true then all Christians have been blessed with salvation through Jesus Christ so that all the earth can be blessed through them. This is why Jesus sends us out (Jn 20:21) to make disciples (Mt 28:18-20), preach the gospel to all (Mk 16:15) and be his witnesses (Acts 1:8).

Questions 9-11. You may want to "prime the pump" by sharing your own list of the ways that God has blessed your own life. Encourage others to share, and then move on to question two: how can God bless others through the resources with which he has blessed you?

The third phase of this question might require some suggestions from you. You might offer some practical ways that God can bless "other nations" through you like (1) supporting an orphan, a missionary or an international ministry through your financial blessings; (2) using your resources of time by becoming an informed prayer partner with an international ministry; (3) offering to use your skills in serving others by teaching English to foreign language speakers or joining a short-term mission service project.

Hearing God's "call" is a wide-open topic. You may want to prepare your own testimony on how you understand God's call on your own life, or you may want to invite a group member to share his or her sense of call. With this question it's also wise to have a book or two on "discerning God's will" to recommend.

Remember that not everyone in the Scriptures received the same audible call as Abram. Paul did on the Damascus Road (Acts 9) and in the Macedonian vision (Acts 16:9), but the call of Paul and Barnabas as missionaries came through a church prayer meeting (Acts 13:1-4). Moses moved purposefully ahead and prayed, in effect, "God, this is where we're going; if you're not with us, please stop us" (Ex 33:18), and Nehemiah saw a need (rebuilding the wall) and rose up to meet that need.

The best thing you can do here is ask the question "How can we put ourselves in a position so that we will hear God's voice—through his Word, Spirit, people and sovereignly orchestrated events?"

Now or Later. This psalm, which constitutes a prayer for an abundant harvest, succinctly repeats the "blessed to be a blessing" theme of God's promises to Abram. There's nothing wrong with asking for God's blessing—as long as we ask so that others, not just ourselves, are blessed.

You might close this study by reading this psalm aloud.

Study 3. The Lord Reigns. Psalm 96.

Purpose: To show that God alone—the Lord of salvation, the nations and all creation—is the worthy focus of our worship.

General note. The Old and New Testament alike declare that God alone is the true God (Ex 20:3-4; Deut 6:4; Jn 14:6; Acts 4:12; 1 Tim 2:5). This truth stands as the foundation of our perspective on our faith in relationship to the world because as we realize the uniqueness of our Lord; we realize that we have a Savior to declare to the nations.

Psalm 96 illustrates how worship and missions go hand in hand. The more we worship God as he is, the more we see his unique and exquisite glory in the world. The more we declare his glory through our worship-filled lives, the more others will have an opportunity to respond and join in the celebration.

Question 1. The psalmist sees God's glory in the fact that he not only has created the universe but also relates to his creation (vv. 11-13). The psalmist sees God as fair, holy and righteous, and stands in awe at the fearful reality of the coming judgment (vv. 10, 13). God is Lord over all peoples and nations (vv. 1-3), supreme over all other deities (vv. 4-5) and worthy of our worship, praise, offerings and prayers.

The phrase "splendor and majesty" in verse 6 would be understood by Old Testament readers as a reference to God's raiment "clothed in splendor and majesty" (Ps 104:1). This serves as an anthropomorphism—an attempt to describe God in human terms (like the phrase "hand of God" to depict God's power). It's saying, "If God wore clothes, they would be indescribable."

Question 2. Psalm 96:1-3 makes up the first of five stanzas in this psalm (1-3, 4-6, 7-9, 10, 11-13). The psalmist calls us to action with the imperatives to *sing, praise, proclaim* and *declare.*

The worship of stanza one focuses on God's name (v. 2) and his works (salvation [v. 2] and deeds [v. 3]). When biblical writers refer to God's "name," it's bigger than just a title. "Name" refers to his revealed character. "Praising his name" could include all sorts of praise to God for his character and attributes such as those the psalm later indicates: Creator, Savior, power, glory, holiness, justice, righteousness, truth and omnipotence.

Our praise focuses on these same attributes and what they mean to us personally, as well as what they have meant throughout Christian history. Applying the imperatives to sing, praise, proclaim and declare may not come easily to us. Make suggestions out of your own daily life as to how you worship throughout the mundane activities of the day or how you seek to proclaim or declare God's glory through your testimony to your peers, teachers or coworkers.

Question 3. Perhaps reflecting on the threefold mandate to "ascribe glory to God" in Psalm 29, the psalmist repeats the phrases here. In light of God's greatness, we simply worship by saying things that are true about almighty God ("the glory due his name," Ps 29:2; 96:8).

When we use the term *worthy* in our worship, we acknowledge that all worth, value and substance lie in God alone. Humans are worshiping beings, and if we fail to worship the true God, we will run after idols we make with our own hands or in our own minds. True worship is simply joining the psalmist and stating, "Yes, Lord, you are awesome, the one-and-only, the Lord of the nations, the judge of all time. We bow down."

The question might arise, "Isn't God egotistical to demand our worship?" The Old Testament phrase about God's being "jealous" to receive our worship provokes such a question. God doesn't need our worship because he's egotistical or insecure. He wants our worship because he loves truth. If he alone is Creator and the source of life, it grieves him when we pursue falsehood by "ascribing glory" to something or someone that is not the truth.

Question 4. "Proclaiming God's salvation" can have two meanings in practical, daily living. On a large scale, it's a call to evangelize the nations of the world. The imperative tells us, "Get out there and announce it from the hilltops that there is a gracious God who wants a relationship with you and will provide a way to give it to you free!"

On a smaller scale, it's also in line with other commands to remember God's works. In other words, this passages exhorts us to get in the habit of daily celebrating all of the big and small ways the reality of God's salvation becomes evident in everyday life.

The mandate also highlights that our evangelism is not something reserved for special events, "evangelistic visitation nights" or special mission endeavors. It's supposed to be a day-after-day thing, a part of everyday life.

Questions 5-6. Expect some lively discussion here, especially regarding the apparent "haughtiness" of a faith that says everyone else's gods are idols. The main point of this question, however, stands against the pluralistic spirit of our age. The goal is to help group members realize that this spirit contradicts the biblical teaching on the absolute uniqueness and exclusivity of the triune God.

As tough as it is for us to accept in our pluralistic, politically correct world, the psalmist calls all other gods "idols." The literal word we translate as "idols" means "nothings": they don't exist; they're human creations.

To illustrate the God versus the "other gods" battle, a quick read through 1 Kings 18:1-46 demonstrates God's power over the false god Baal.

Yahweh, the God of the Bible, sets himself apart as majestic Creator. Other psalms that celebrate the worship of God as Lord of creation include 19, 33 and 104. The challenge in our time is to understand how to address people of other religions and worldviews with respect while nonetheless holding to the exclusivity of the biblical God, revealed to us through Jesus Christ. Two things you can do in response are (1) read through Acts 17 to observe Paul's respectful but confrontational reaction to the false gods of the people on Mars Hill; and (2) consult Ajith Fernando's *A Christian Attitude Toward World Religions* for a perspective from a Christian leader in a Buddhist and Hindu country.

Question 7. Verses 11-13 refer to creation's celebration in relationship to God. They provoke the question "When will this happen?" Christian scholars take two divergent views. We know that "creation groans" and has been affected by sin's accumulated impact (see Rom 8:19-21), but does this mean that the rejoicing heavens and seas and trees sing only after Jesus comes as judge?

Some take this view, relegating this celebration to a time after the judgment of God has established a new millennial kingdom on earth. Others think the verses illustrate the ongoing anticipation of creation—which indicates that even today we can see creation as part of the worship chorus of God.

People who take the former view often struggle with appreciating the natural world, because they see its decay as simply a natural progression toward judgment day. The latter position opens the doors wide for allowing God's created world to join us in worship. The ocean tides sing of God's power and faithfulness. The songbirds often lift voices in praise that God alone hears. The majestic mountains stand in testimony of God's power.

Question 8. In keeping with God's absolute devotion to truth, he desires that all the "families of the nations" and "all the earth" (vv. 7, 9) will worship him in the splendor of his holiness. John Piper, in his book *Let the Nations Be Glad,* illustrates the relationship between worship and missions this way: "Missions exists because worship doesn't. . . . Worship, therefore, is the fuel and goal in missions. It's the goal of missions because in missions we simply aim to bring the nations into the white-hot enjoyment of God's glory. The goal of missions is the gladness of the peoples in the greatness of God.

"But worship is also the fuel of missions. Passion for God in worship precedes the offer of God in preaching. You cannot commend what you don't cherish. Missionaries will never call out 'Let the nations be glad!' who cannot say from the heart, 'I rejoice in the Lord. . . . I will be glad and exult in thee, I will sing praise to thy name, O Most High' (Ps 104:34; 9:2). Missions begins and ends in worship" ([Grand Rapids, Baker, 1993], p. 11).

Question 9. The reality of God's judgment is a very powerful theme in the Bible and has historically been a large motivational factor in the desire to spread God's Word. Ezekiel wrote of the ministry of warning others (Ezek 3:17-19), while Jude wrote of showing mercy with fear so as to "snatch others from the fire and save them" (Jude 23). Paul the apostle understood the reality of judgment when he wrote that the "wages of sin is death" (Rom 6:23); in light of this compelling message, he stated, "Woe is me if I do not preach the gospel" (1 Cor 9:16).

Hudson Taylor's image of millions of Chinese plunging into the bottomless chasm of a Christless eternity drove him into the interior of China with the China Inland Mission over a hundred years ago. A. B. Simpson's understanding of people without Christ caused him to pray over a globe, letting his tears of compassion fall on countries like Vietnam and Cambodia. The denomination he founded, the Christian and Missionary Alliance, sent out many missionaries to these locations—because they believed in the awesomeness of God's grace and the awfulness of God's judgment.

The bottom-line teaching of Scripture can be summarized this way: If the wonderful news of grace and eternal life does not thrust us out in outreach and missions, then how about the terrible news of God's coming judgment? For he is coming to judge the earth (Ps 96:13).

Question 10. Encourage the group to think through "global opportunities" right where you live like: praying for the countries on the labels of your clothes, praying through international issues in the news, getting involved in English as a Second Language (ESL) classes, visiting and getting to know local people from other world religions, building friendships with owners of foreign-food restaurants, getting involved in international student ministry, inviting a ethnically different neighbor over for a meal.

Now or Later. Why is it "too small a thing" for God to be concerned only about the restoration of the people of Israel? Simply put, he is God of the nations—not just the "tribal deity" of the Israelites.

56 ────────────────────────────────── *Missions*

Study 4. God's Attack on Racism. Jonah 1—4.

Purpose: To show that God's mercy exceeds our hostility toward others. Therefore, understanding God's mercy helps us overcome fear, prejudice and hatred.

General note. Jonah is not the story of a man fearfully running from obedience. It is the story of a man defying God's compassion, a man who ran so he didn't have to demonstrate God's compassion to his enemies. W. Graham Scroggie summarizes it this way: "The object of the book of Jonah seems to have been to correct the extreme form of Jewish nationalism which then prevailed, and to proclaim the mercy of God for the Gentiles as well as for the Jews" (*Know Your Bible* [London: Pickering & Inglis, 1972], p. 159).

Question 1. Jonah was a Jewish prophet, son of Amittai, from the city called Gath Hepher in Zebulun (2 Kings 14:25) about three miles from Nazareth. He lived in the period 825-782 B.C., under the reign of Jeroboam II (2 Kings 14:27) in the northern kingdom, before the great exile. His contemporaries were prophets like Joel, Hosea and Amos.

At this time Israel hated Assyria, the empire in which Nineveh was the capital. Nineveh sat on the Tigris River near the modern-day city of Mosul, Iraq. For three hundred years Assyria was a brutally militaristic empire known and hated by all its West Asian neighbors for its violence, conquests and reputation for cannibalizing defeated foes.

Jonah sailed from Joppa (modern-day Jaffa, about thirty miles northwest of Jerusalem) toward Tarshish, what scholars identify as the city of Tartessus in southwestern Spain, a city over two thousand miles from Jonah's home and in the opposite direction of Nineveh. Chapters 1 and 2 don't tell us why he ran, other than the fact that he "ran away from the Lord" (1:3). Fear of Ninevites seems at first to be the logical reason.

Question 2. In contrast to the panicking sailors, Jonah fell into a deep sleep during the storm. It could have been the sleep of depression, because Jonah, a prophet, was now out of work. Maybe he didn't care if the ship sank. On the other hand, it could be the sleep of denial. Perhaps getting on the boat was not escape enough from God so Jonah ran away even further through his sleep.

The sailors call Jonah to prayer, but we don't know if he prayed. His own understanding of his relationship with God would have rendered his prayers useless because he knew that conscious sin, like his flight to Tarshish, separated him from talking to God (Ps 66:18; Is 59:2).

The lot gets cast—an ancient means of divination, like throwing dice—to identify the person responsible for the storm, and it falls to Jonah. He offers his testimony about his God (1:9) and reiterates something he apparently told them earlier—that he was a fugitive from God (1:10).

Question 3. As the seas rise, Jonah shows his capacity for mercy by offering a prompt solution: "Throw me into the sea" (1:12). Even in Jonah's disobedience, God uses him to bring these pagan sailors to call on the name of Jonah's God (1:14), and they offer a sacrifice (1:16).

Question 4. Jonah's prayer vividly describes the experiences of someone who has almost drowned ("heart of the seas," "currents," "waves," "breakers," "engulfing waters," "seaweed"). The theme of his prayer focuses on (1) God's compassion—he is near to the needy; (2) God's use of hardships (note "your waves and breakers" [2:3]) to bring us to himself, an important truth for any of us who ever ask, "Why does God let me go through these things?" God uses pain to get our attention! (3) God's love in spite of how we feel, because circumstances can make us feel like God has abandoned us; and (4) God's mercy—God still redeems. Salvation comes from the Lord!

Question 5. In 2:9 Jonah is saying, "If you get me out of here, I'll go to Nineveh." You might use this to provoke discussion on the "vows" we make under pressure.

Question 6. The main thing to emphasize here is that God is the God of the second, third, fiftieth and five hundredth chance! Certainly there may be time needed for healing after rebelling against God, but God does not "shelve" repentant, forgiven sinners. The only biblical reason for getting left on the "shelf" would be the unforgivable sin, blaspheming the Holy Spirit, which most interpret as lifelong rejection of Christ (Mt 12:31).

Questions 7-8. Jonah obeys (3:3) and goes to Nineveh. Keep in mind the inconvenience. He was sailing in comfort to Tarshish, asleep in the boat. To get to Nineveh, Jonah had to travel more than five hundred miles over land, desert and mountains. He would have had many opportunities to reconsider, rationalize and run again—but he went.

Nineveh and the surrounding metropolitan region was a huge city, three days' walk across. Jonah declares the message of warning and judgment: "In forty days Nineveh will be destroyed" (3:4). The Assyrian Empire, proud and haughty, represented heathen defiance against the God of Israel, but here they listen to Jonah. His succinct message affects everyone, all the way up to the king, who declares a fast for repentance. From a prophetic perspective—

especially in contrast to some of his peers—Jonah succeeds. (It's worth noting that Assyrian pride later returned, and God destroyed Nineveh in the seventh century B.C.; but here, they repent.)

Question 9. The second call gets gentler, although Jonah's message is harsh. Perhaps God knew of Jonah's hatred of the Ninevites so he invited him to condemn Nineveh (1:3). But Jonah knew God's character (4:2), which God substantiates by having mercy and sparing Nineveh and its people (3:10).

Question 10. Jonah 4:2 relates the real reason Jonah ran. John Piper writes, "[Jonah] tried to run away because he knew God would be gracious to the people and forgive them. The point of the book is not the fish. It's about missions and racism and ethnocentrism. The point is this: be merciful like God, not miserly like Jonah. For Jonah 'be merciful' meant to be a missionary" (Piper, *Let the Nations,* p. 188).

Jonah 4:5 implies that Jonah was still longing for God's judgment on Nineveh. He sat on the hill and watched—hoping for the hellfire and brimstone to fall as they had on Sodom and Gomorrah (Gen 19:24).

Question 11. God's mercy in this book is not just for the Ninevites but for Jonah as well. God takes care of Jonah by teaching him through these parables. God provides the plant for protection, but he sends the worm and the wind to remind Jonah (and us) that he cares more for our growth than he does for our comfort.

Question 12. You may want to provide a quiet moment for group members to reflect on this question, but before you do, remind them that the Israelite hatred of Nineveh in Jonah's time would parallel twentieth-century Jews' hatred of Nazis. Our love for our enemies must flow from our understanding of God's mercy toward us.

Question 13. Jonah's story answers two basic questions concerning how God's mercy sends us out in missionary service. First, this account speaks to the question "Do I have to love every person before I share the gospel with them?" Jonah's answer is "No. All you need is to know God's mercy yourself."

A missionary preparing for Bible translation with an ethnic group in West Africa was asked, "How did you come to love these people?"

The man shocked the audience by replying, "I don't love these people." Then he continued, "I know that Jesus loves me, and Jesus loves these people, and I pray that I'll come to love them. But I'm not going because I love them. I'm going because I've experienced God's mercy through Jesus Christ, and I want them to have the same opportunity to receive God's mercy in Christ."

The second question Jonah answers goes like this: "Why should I go to those outside of Christ? Won't I just be increasing their accountability and judgment?" In other words, if people have no knowledge of Christ, shouldn't we just leave them alone in hope that they can live up to the "light" they have? Do we condemn them to hell if we proclaim Christ and they reject him?

By no means! The people of Nineveh were condemned already—just as people without Christ have no Savior to cover their sins. Jonah illustrates that unless the messengers of God go, the people will have no chance at all. God does not send Jonah simply to condemn, but in compassion God sends Jonah in order to give people already under judgment the opportunity to respond, repent and be saved.

And that's why he sends us—to give people under the judgment of their own sins a chance to respond to his compassion demonstrated in the sacrificial death of Jesus Christ. We go—like Jonah—with bad news and good news. God is holy and condemns sin. But God is compassionate and longs for repentant sinners to respond to his love.

Now or Later. Through his encounter with the Samaritan woman at the well, Jesus illustrates to the disciples that his mercy transcends cultural and ethnic stereotypes. Encourage group members to read this story in the week ahead, especially because outreach to "Samaria" is part of the next lesson's "concentric circle outreach."

Study 5. Concentric-Circle Outreach. Acts 1:1-11.

Purpose: To show that God's heart for the world is played out through us, empowered by the Holy Spirit as his witnesses, going out globally.

General note. Luke, a Gentile (non-Jewish) believer in Christ, got very excited about the global implications of the gospel of Jesus Christ. He writes about the spread of the gospel in the book of Acts. In these introductory verses, he outlines the outward-rippling outreach of the church that he'll describe in detail in the chapters that follow.

Question 2. Jesus told his disciples that he was going to send what his Father had promised so that they could be "clothed with power from on high" (Lk 24:49). Luke repeats this command to "wait" for the promised gift. The questions that follow indicate that the disciples really had no idea what Jesus was talking about. Their religious background offered little understanding of the ministry of the Holy Spirit.

The only specific command Jesus gave was to wait in Jerusalem. After their dramatic failure of abandoning him at the cross, they might have been tempted to head for home after Jesus ascended into heaven. They later interpreted his command to "wait" as an imperative to pray (Acts 1:14), but this probably demonstrated only that they were helpless and confused.

Question 3. Luke's first volume, written to this same Theophilus, intended to present an "orderly account" of the ministry of Jesus so that Theophilus might believe with "certainty" (Lk 1:3-4). Here Luke picks up on Jesus' work through the Spirit after his resurrection. He writes to remind Theophilus and the other readers that Jesus' work continued after his resurrection and ascension.

The question "Who is Theophilus?" may arise. The name means "friend of God" or "lover of God." Some conjecture it was not one person but rather the community of believers. Others point to Luke's addressing him as the "most excellent" (Lk 1:3), which could indicate that he was a Roman official.

Question 4. The concept "kingdom of God," which Jesus addressed in the forty days between the resurrection and the ascension, usually refers to the presence of God in various forms: his people, his Spirit, Jesus himself or even heaven (the eternal kingdom).

The disciples, Israelites living under the oppression of the Roman government, interpreted the "kingdom of God" as the restoration of the kingdom to Israel with Jesus presumably as king. These political aspirations provoked the "Hosanna" worship of the triumphal entry (Jn 12:12-19). Some theorize that Judas's betrayal was his way of forcing Jesus to overthrow the Roman powers that came to take him.

The intentions of the disciples in contrast to Jesus' kingdom plans provides a good foundation for the group to discuss the question "In what ways do we, like these disciples, try to use Jesus for our purposes rather than hearing his?"

Question 5. Jesus wants people to focus on being his witnesses rather than on the specific details of his second coming.

This verse (as well as vv. 9-11) may provoke some discussion about Jesus' second coming and the end of the world. It's important to affirm the only things we can be *sure* that the Scriptures teach: (a) Jesus definitely is coming back, (b) he's coming suddenly, (c) he's coming visibly, and (d) he's coming to end human history as we know it. Church history demonstrates that preoccupation with the specific nuances of the end times often divides the church or at least distracts us from Jesus' mandate to be his witnesses. The church, like those apostles, finds itself standing around gazing into heaven.

Question 6. Keep in mind the awful feeling of failure that must have plagued these disciples. They had abandoned Jesus in his hour of greatest need, even to the point of denying any knowledge of him. Now they had seen the resurrected Jesus, which absolutely proved his power over death. But they were acutely aware of their own lack of power. Jesus' promise states in effect, "The power that raised me from the dead is available to you."

Use this discussion of power to invite people to talk about their own experiences of feeling powerless like these disciples and needing the Holy Spirit's power. The resurrection power of Jesus gives us ability to overcome failure, fear and inadequacy.

Questions 7 and 10. For the disciples "Jerusalem" was their immediate locale, although as Galileans they would not be confident there. They were peasants in Israel's most sophisticated city. Their recent failure in standing strong with Christ underscored their need for power.

"Judea" would represent their own ethnic group scattered across the nation. "Samaria" constitutes arguably the most controversial locale because Jews grew up hating the Samaritans—ethnic "half-breeds" (see Jn 4; Acts 8). To us they represent people who live geographically close but remain culturally separated from our own people.

The "ends of the earth" to these listeners represented Rome—which is why Luke's account in Acts begins in Jerusalem (Acts 1—7), ripples out to Judea and Samaria (Acts 8ff.), and concludes in Rome (Acts 28:17ff.).

Two other words are worth noting in Acts 1:8. The words for "power" and "witnesses" provide color to the text. The Greek word for power (*dynamis*) is the word from which we also get "dynamite" and "dynamo." Jesus is talking about explosive power, the power that raised him from the dead and created the universe! The Greek word for witness (*martyria*) is the word from which we get "martyr," indicating the intensity of the cost of being a witness in that first century. To be Christ's witnesses meant being faithful—even unto death!

Question 8. See the note above on question 5. In some way Jesus will descend back to earth to bring the world as we know it to an end. You may want to pause here and have someone read 1 Thessalonians 4:16-18.

Question 9. It's important to note the progression here: we wait, we receive power after the Holy Spirit comes on us, and then we become witnesses to the gospel locally, crossculturally and to the ends of the earth. This power gives us boldness to witness and victory over fear (see Acts 4:31; 2 Tim 1:7). The daily power enables us to live obedient lives (Eph 5:18). Trying to live the Christian life as Jesus' witnesses in our own strength is a vain exercise in frustration.

Inviting dialogue on the Holy Spirit can get the group into a variety of topics, especially related to individuals' experiences with spiritual power. To avoid unnecessary conflict and to keep any one person's subjective experiences from overtaking the discussion, try to focus on the text in Acts by evaluating every experience of power with the question "In keeping with Jesus' promise in Acts 1:8, how did this experience strengthen your witness?"

Question 10. You may want to prompt this discussion by sharing examples from your own life over the past week. See also notes for question 6.

Now or Later. Note that the church stayed in their Jerusalem "comfort zone" until God, through a great persecution, thrust them out. Ask group members to consider what it might take for God to thrust them out.

Study 6. Ambassadors for Christ. 2 Corinthians 5:11-21.

Purpose: To demonstrate that we serve as Christ's ambassadors of reconciliation to the world based on all that Jesus Christ has done for us on the cross.

General note. This passage finds us in the midst of Paul's discussion of what motivates us to minister to others. Everything we do is in the context of a heavenly vision (2 Cor 5:2, 6), and our compelling motivation is to be pleasing to Jesus (2 Cor 5:9). In these verses, Paul describes what motivates such absolute devotion to the Lord.

Question 1. Some, especially those unfamiliar with biblical language, may find it odd to read that Paul found motivation for witness in the "fear" of the Lord (2 Cor 5:11). Try explaining the difference between fear (that is, respect) of God and being afraid of God (Prov 9:10; Acts 5:11). But also emphasize that Paul's sense of rendering an account (2 Cor 5:10) provoked this sense of trembling before God, along the lines of James 3:1.

Paul's sense of being a sinner loved by God (5:14) also motivated him. He was "compelled" because he realized that his life was a response to the gracious and undeserved sacrifice of Christ. Refer to 2 Corinthians 5:21 throughout this study as the summation of the work of Christ's demonstrated love for us.

Paul's awe at God's greatness as Creator and Judge (fear) as well as God's love and grace demonstrated in Jesus' death on the cross combined for him into what Oswald Chambers called "the determination to serve." Reading Chambers's February 24 entry in *My Utmost for His Highest* can help you illustrate the motives that drove Paul the apostle.

Question 2. The death of Christ on the cross does not get relegated to some theological truth with no connection to daily living. Jesus died so that he might bring his followers into the experience of unselfish living.

The death and resurrection of Jesus Christ lead us to live for others. We live a Christ-imitating life that says through daily behavior, "My life was given so that you might benefit." It's worth pausing here to ask a few practical questions like "If Christ died so that I might no longer live for myself alone, how will this affect my driving . . . work . . . treatment of others . . . relationship to my parents . . . parenting decisions . . . financial decisions?"

Question 3. The second part of the verse refers to Paul's preconversion view of Christ. Before he was made new through rebirth in Christ (5:17), Paul regarded Jesus as only a human being, a mere mortal teacher. Paul's conversion caused him to change his entire outlook on Jesus.

Applied to the way we look at others, the phrase could have two related meanings. First, it could mean that because at our conversion we change the way we look at Christ, we also allow him to change the way we look at others. Our transformation in Christ causes us to look at others and say, "This person is created in the image of God and is someone who deserves to hear the message of God in Christ."

A second meaning could relate to looking at others from an eternal point of view. In other words, we lose our this-world-only outlook on others, and we start to see them as human beings with eternal spirits that will stand in judgment before almighty God.

Question 4. God initiates reconciliation (v. 21) and provides Jesus as the payment for our sins so that we can be restored to right relationship with him. In light of the cross, God no longer holds our sins against us (v. 18).

Help the group to understand this by underscoring the complete message of the gospel, especially by reviewing the summary in verse 21. God, in his holiness, burns with righteous anger against us for our sins (Rom 3:23). For reconciliation to occur, we (or our substitute) must pay the penalty that our sins deserve, namely, death (Rom 6:23). God purchased our reconciliation through Jesus' death on the cross by making Jesus our substitute. John uses the word *propitiation* (1 Jn 4:10), which means the satisfaction of God's wrath. Why? So that we might become the "righteousness of God" (v. 21) through him.

This passage raises the issue of human sinfulness and our inability to find our way back to God. Some will resist this idea, thinking that reconciliation is our pursuit of God. Romans 3 clearly indicates, however, that God pursues us because we stand spiritually helpless and lost in our sins. Understanding our complete and utter lostness requires humility. But when we, in humility, realize the extent to which God went to bring us back, we understand why the gospel is good news. Then we say with Paul, in response to this news, "the love of Christ compels us." This response motivates our witness as his "ambassadors."

Question 5. Emphasize here our responsiveness to God's love. We don't do outward ministry to earn God's love but rather in response to that love, which makes us into new people who are reconciled to God.

Since many Christians struggle with the desire to earn God's love through good deeds, provoke the discussion a little further by asking, "How can we tell if we're going out in ministry in response to what Jesus has done for us rather than in an attempt to earn God's love?"

Question 6. 2 Corinthians 5:21 is the foundation on which our witness to the world is built. Because God reconciled us to himself through Christ, we now have this ministry and message of reconciliation.

The *ministry* of reconciliation pertains to our relationships. In light of God's reconciliatory relationship toward us, we look to be peacemakers with others (Mt 5:7), helping reconcile people back to God and to each other.

The *message* of reconciliation relates to our proclamation that God, in Christ, was changing things so that we are no longer God's enemies (Rom 5:10) but rather are "savable" through Christ's work. Our desire to see people returned to a right relationship with God causes us to cry out to others, "Be reconciled to God" (that is, accept the gift God is offering) (2 Cor 5:20).

Question 7. An ambassador does not speak on his or her own behalf. He or she goes as an emissary of a head of state to bring an important message. As "ambassadors" for Christ, we go into each day with a message from the King of kings.

Being an ambassador can change the way we look at ourselves. Ask the group, "If you went into each new day with the phrase 'I am an ambassador of the king' on your lips, how would it affect the way that you enter your workplace, classroom or neighborhood?"

Question 8. Remember the earlier discussion which asserted that the motive for evangelism comes from both the anticipation of eternity and the sobering awfulness of eternal judgment.

Question 9. Here's where our responsibility as witnesses for Christ strikes us hardest. God "making his appeal" through us certainly indicates that his divine method for getting the message out to others is through our witness.

Affirm here that while God alone does the work of conversion (therefore, we don't need to worry that we have to do everything "just right" in order to win people to Christ), we do bear the responsibility of getting the word out. God alone can bring someone into his family, but we are responsible to deliver his invitations. We go out as ambassadors stating, "the King of the universe desires an audience with you." Failing to speak means we're avoiding our ambassadorial responsibility.

Question 10. Self-image goes hand in hand with being effective witnesses. Remember to affirm that being a "new creation" in Christ provides the framework and the foundation for our evangelistic witness.

Now or Later. This is the story of Isaiah's call. Encourage others to note especially the progression: worship and awe at the holiness of God, a sense of lostness, an experience of being reconciled, and a calling to go out as God's ambassador.

Study 7. The Motivational Example. Philippians 2:1-11.

Purpose: To present the incarnational example of Jesus Christ as our source of sustained motivation for endurance in the face of the loss of comforts and sacrifice of personal rights which accompany service.

General note. Philippians falls into the Prison Epistle category because Paul wrote it from some sort of captivity. This letter is distinguished by the word *joy,* with at least fourteen references to *joy* or *rejoice.* One commentator stated, "Joy is the music of Philippians."

From this joy-in-spite-of-the-circumstances context, Paul exhorts his readers to imitate the example of Jesus. He quotes in chapter 2 from what was probably a hymn in the early church (2:6-11) about the *kenosis* (or "emptying," "he made himself nothing," [v. 7]) of Jesus.

Question 1. Philippians 2:1-4 introduces the context from which Paul exhorts his readers to imitate Jesus. He challenges the readers toward unity, fellowship, tenderness and compassion. Evidently there were rifts in the church at Philippi (see Phil 4:2-3), and the believers were anything but "like-minded" or "one in spirit and purpose." Therefore Paul stirs his readers to think of others as better than themselves and serve accordingly. He then points to the selfless example of Jesus as the ultimate illustration.

Question 2. Throughout, the Bible teaches the principle of inverted greatness. If you want to be first, be last. If you want to be greatest, become the least. If you want to be a master, become a servant. Jesus' own life personifies this principle, which Bill Hybels calls "descending into greatness."

He was in every way God (Jn 1:1-5), but he released this greatness to come serve. He went past the point of mere identification; he died the death that we deserve (2 Cor 5:21) and paid the penalty for our sins on the cross (Is 53:6). From humility Jesus is exalted and rewarded for his faithful obedience, as in 1 Peter 5:6.

This passage might provoke other questions for further study. The "being in very nature God" and the "made himself nothing" references will inevitably provoke the question "If Jesus is fully God, how did God separate himself from God?" Probably the best response is something like this: "I really don't know; this falls into the category of the 'mystery' of the Trinity. For our purposes, it's enough to see that Jesus gave up heavenly power and privileges to become a human being—an overwhelming sacrifice to show his love for us."

Question 3. Philippians tells us that Jesus released his heavenly privileges (v. 6) and became "nothing." He became a servant even to the point of washing his disciples' feet, including the feet of his betrayer, Judas (Jn 13). He suffered the difficulties and temptations of the human existence, yet without sin (Heb 4:15). And then he suffered the indignities of beating, persecution, ridicule, torture, nakedness and death on the cross.

Why did Jesus do all this? Philippians 2:8 tells us that Jesus' motive was obedience. Other passages remind us that this obedience to his God-given mission (Jn 1:29) was love (Jn 3:16; 1 Jn 3:16).

If it relates well to your small group, listening to or reading the words of Joan Osborne's song "What If God Was One of Us?" could provoke good discussion. Ask, "If Joan were here right now, how would you respond to her out of Philippians 2:6-8?"

Question 4. The passage does indicate that Jesus chose to come to earth, to serve and to die. Group members might respond, "Sacrifices I choose are always easier than sacrifices that have been thrust into my life—like a handicap, an abusive relationship or economic hardship."

To apply this passage, remind people that Jesus' choices were always in creative tension with God's "call." Did Jesus choose to die on the cross? Yes. But he did it out of obedience (v. 8), and we know that he resisted it and asked God to do it another way (Lk 22:42). Jesus chose to come to earth, but he still learned obedience through the things he suffered (Heb 5:8).

When we find ourselves living under hardships we didn't choose, we are still exhorted to imitate Jesus, to choose joy (as Paul was doing in the Philippian imprisonment) and to learn contentment (as Paul illustrates in Phil 4:11).

Question 5. Remind people of the seeking God who goes after lost people with his inquiring question "Where are you?" Get them thinking about social or economic or political worlds which need to be penetrated with Christ's love through our presence.

What worlds around us remain untouched with the love of Christ because God's people refuse to go in? the economically poor? HIV/AIDS patients? prisoners? bankers? university faculty? actors? other-language speakers?

Question 6. To understand Paul's perspective, look at Philippians 1:12-18 to see how he saw his chains as an opportunity to spread the gospel, even to his Roman guards. Consider his motivation as expressed in Philippians 1:21, where identification with Christ is his greatest desire.

Going beyond Paul alone, consider also the apostles in Acts who faced hardship "rejoicing because they had been counted worthy of suffering for the Name" (Acts 5:41). You might want to include here the words of the missionary C. T. Studd, who recruited people to service in India, China and Africa with the mandate "If Christ be God and died for me, no sacrifice I make is too great."

Question 7. People can misapply this verse in one of two ways. On the one hand some will think, *I must become nothing; I must give and give and never think about my needs and feelings. I must burn myself out in service to others.*

At the other extreme some will read this verse and think, *I have multiple needs, a difficult past and lots of unresolved issues; I can never get past them. I can never be that selfless.*

Remind the first group that Philippians 2:4 does not exhort us to ignore our own needs; it simply says that we should not focus *only* on our own needs but also on the needs of others. Burning out has no inherent merit; long-term faithfulness yields a much greater impact.

Bring the second group back to the biblical truth that we often find healing by giving to others. We must address preoccupation with selfish needs because it contradicts Philippians 2:3-4. Reminding people that when we give ourselves away we find ourselves, however, might provide a better incentive to imitate Jesus.

Question 8. The biblical perspective contradicts the "this world" orientation of our culture. While our world tells us to live for today, God exhorts us to a longer view. The Bible teaches that sufferings in this life are incomparable to the rewards in the next (2 Cor 4:16-18). It tells us to live as citizens of heaven (Phil 3:20) and to endure whatever hardships accompany our citizenship.

The "sacrifice-now, reward-later" principle is incredibly important when considering the costs that will be required to bring the gospel to unreached people in the hard places of the world. But the Bible consistently affirms that sacrifice now yields fruit later—both in this life and the next. Jesus himself summarized his ministry by stating, "Unless a kernel of wheat falls to the ground and dies, it remains only a single seed. But if it dies, it produces many seeds" (Jn 12:24).

Question 9. Continuing this theme of sacrifice, this question points to motivation. Should we endure because we have rewards ahead? Did Jesus? The text does not specifically indicate that Jesus endured the cross (v. 8) because he anticipated the reward ahead (vv. 9-11), but other passages certainly do. Hebrews 12:2 reminds us that Jesus endured the cross "for the joy set before him."

In the same way, Paul could manifest joy in prison because of the anticipation of being in Christ's presence (Phil 1:23), and he endured another prison cell by focusing on the anticipated "crown of righteousness" ahead (2 Tim 4:8).

Philip Yancey summarized the motivational power of the eternal perspective in his *Christianity Today* column: "For years all the New Testament talk about eternal rewards embarrassed me. Now, I see eternal rewards as the ultimate form of delayed gratification. Why do missionary relief workers volunteer for hellish places like Somalia, Rwanda, and the Sudan? I have interviewed these workers, and among other motives they mention the prospect of reward. They hope to hear someday, 'Well done, thou good and faithful servant'" (February 5, 1996, p. 112).

Question 10. Philippians 2:5-11 provides wonderful incentive for short-term missions. Raising our own money in an effort to go and serve others directly imitates the example of Jesus. Philippians 2:6-8 illustrates that Jesus paid to serve us. If our attitude of service is the same as his (2:5), shouldn't we likewise be willing to pay for the opportunity to serve others?

Study 8. Eyes on the Prize. Hebrews 11:1—12:3.

Purpose: To show that we're part of a long legacy of the people of God who made a dramatic impact through their faith, eternal perspective and endurance.

General note. The "hall of fame" of faith reminds us of three truths about God's work. (1) God uses sinners who, by faith, put their trust in him. (2) God's people win great victories and suffer immensely in his service. (3) The common thread in God's work through his people is the long-term view: "looking forward to the city . . . whose architect and builder is God" (11:10).

Question 1. The strong statement that faith is both "assurance" and "certainty" will inevitably provoke discussion about the struggle that we all have with doubt. The "ancients" (that is, the Old Testament patriarchs) were commended for their unwavering faith (11:2), but many of us don't feel so certain about things "hoped for" and "unseen."

One helpful story which illustrates our struggle appears in Mark 9 where a father yearns for his son's deliverance from an evil spirit. Jesus tells him that everything is possible for him who believes. The father replies, "I do believe; help me overcome my unbelief" (Mk 9:23-24). Even though this father struggled with doubt, Jesus healed the boy.

In the same way, God can work to help us overcome our doubts. It also helps to note that faith in the Bible is more a choice of the spirit than it is a feeling. We tend to relegate faith to a feeling of confidence, whereas the Bible regards it as a choice we make. "So we fix our eyes not on what is seen but on what is unseen. For what is seen is temporary, but what is unseen is eternal" (2 Cor 4:18). This idea of an intentional choice to focus on the certainty of an unseen future carries through the examples of Hebrews 11.

Question 2. Pleasing faith affirms God's unique existence and focuses our hope on God as the great rewarder. Note here that staying focused on God and his work in anticipation of a reward is okay with God. As we'll see later in this chapter, the anticipation of reward serves as an intense motivator for faithful obedience (see 2 Tim 4:8).

Question 3. In preparation for this question, you might want to skim through a commentary on Hebrews 11 or a Bible dictionary where you can look up these Old Testament people and become familiar with their lives.

Question 4. Hebrews 11 teaches us that God's use of human lives for his purposes always comes from his grace and mercy. Noah's life included drunkenness and some type of immorality (Gen 9:20-24). Abraham lied twice about Sarah as his wife (Gen 12:17-20; 20:1-13). Moses had a hot temper and lived forty years in exile because he murdered an Egyptian (Ex 2:11). David's adultery led him to deceit and murder (2 Sam 11). Rahab lived as a prostitute. Samson destroyed himself by his own uncontrolled lusts. Gideon doubted God repeatedly.

And yet God used them all. God calls Abraham his "friend," Moses the "meekest man on all the earth" who talked with God face to face, and David a "man after God's own heart."

The question arises, "Should we imitate these people and sin boldly so that God's grace is even more evident in us?" Emphasize that God never endorses the abuse of grace by intentional rebellion, but he always stands ready to forgive the repentant sinner (Lk 18:13).

Question 5. Review the notes from study two concerning the decision that Abraham had to make in being obedient. Hebrews 11 elaborates his decision of faith by underscoring these realities: he was called; he left behind security; he went to a place of uncertainty; he settled in a foreign place without a stable home; he lived in tents, symbolic of the "not-yet-ness" of his life as a stranger on the earth (Gen 23:5); his insecurities here drove him to look to the eternal so that his eyes were focused on a heavenly kingdom.

Question 6. The New Testament saints also lived for heaven—see Paul's comments in Philippians 1:21; 3:20; Romans 14:7-8; Acts 20:24. In Scripture the heavenly vision never excuses our responsibilities as citizens on earth so that we become "so heavenly minded we're no earthly good." Christians must not lose their credibility by keeping their heads in the clouds. The biblical teaching on a heavenly future is designed to keep us courageous and faithful in the midst of hardship. "Therefore we do not lose heart. . . . For our light and momentary troubles are achieving for us an eternal glory that far outweighs them all" (2 Cor 4:16-17). We stay faithful in our service on earth because we believe in the ultimate delayed gratification—the eternal kingdom of Jesus Christ.

Question 7. Invite discussion to see whether or not people have heard of this teaching or seen it on TV. See if you can determine where people are at regarding it.

Then point out from the text that some of the people of Hebrews 11 obeyed God and prospered greatly—like Abraham, David and Solomon. But these concluding verses remind us that for others living by faith cost them their lives. Teachers of the prosperity gospel (that following Jesus guarantees health, wealth and success) usually choose to overlook texts like these as well as Jesus' experience of and teaching about the cross. For the people in Hebrews 11:32-38, what did their faith get them? What did Jesus' faith get him?

As Paul put it to the Philippians, our desire is to know both the power of the resurrection and the fellowship of sharing in his sufferings (Phil 3:10). Prosperity gospel proponents desire only the former.

Question 8. Allow group members to express fears like "If I follow Christ, will he make me go to the slums? be single? be poor?" But remind them that faith is a choice, not a feeling. It's okay to be afraid, but we cannot be ruled by our fears. The psalmist wrote "When [not if] I am afraid, I will trust in you" (Ps 56:3-4). Mary Slessor, the famous nonmarried missionary to West Africa, summarized the faith-versus-fear tension this way: "Courage is the conquering of fear by faith."

Question 9. If group members seem out of touch with the realities of Christians who live in difficult circumstances, you might want to provide some statistics on the persecuted church around the world. Information can be found at websites of groups like Voice of the Martyrs <www.vom.org> or the World Evangelical Fellowship's Religious Liberty Commission <www.wef.org>.

Question 10. It helps here to suggest specific ways to "fix our eyes" on the work of Jesus Christ: memorizing a verse, rereading a passage related to Jesus' crucifixion, meditating on a picture of Jesus' suffering, watching the crucifixion scene in the *Jesus* video.

Question 11. One way to start this discussion is to hand out 3x5 cards with the statement "Because I believe in heaven, I will . . ."

Now or Later. This is a passage on a life with a one-purpose-only focus

Study 9. Diversity in Heaven. Revelation 7:9-14.

Purpose: To see the culmination of God's mission in a global, crosscultural worship service. Through Abraham and his children of faith, all the nations have indeed been blessed by the saving work of Jesus Christ.

General note. Why does God inform us that people from "every nation, tribe, people and language" will be worshiping together in heaven? God celebrates the diversity of culture and ethnicity—to the point that John's heavenly vision indicates that we will still have some aspect of ethnic distinction in heaven.

Question 1. A multinational, multiracial congregation stands together. The crowd is too great to number. The white robes symbolize resurrection glory. The palm branches signify the celebration after a victorious return from battle (Mk 11:8).

The emphasis on white robes may seem offensive to non-Anglos, but you should note that "white" to the Middle Eastern readers of the Bible had nothing to do with skin color. Instead it signified purity and the washing away of sin. The white robes depict the status of the redeemed sinner before God, washed clean by the blood of Christ, no matter what the skin color of this global fellowship.

Question 2. John describes these people as being from every nation, tribe, tongue and language. Did they carry national flags? wear native attire? speak or sing in their mother tongues? We don't know. All we do know is that they carried their cultural distinctiveness with them into the heavenly worship service. Heaven will not be monocultural!

Question 3. The sentence "Salvation belongs to our God . . . and to the Lamb" is the worshipers' way of stating, "The only reason we can stand here is the work of God." They reiterate this theme in verse 12 and throughout the book of Revelation. They know that salvation cannot be earned. They stand as worshipers because of God's grace alone!

Question 4. Jesus is God's sacrificial Lamb, the perfect sacrifice for the sins of the world. Christians familiar with biblical symbols will know this, but newer Christians might not. For them, it might help to read Isaiah 53:6 and John 1:29.

The passage in Revelation 5:8-10 asserts that these people from every tribe, language, people and nation have been purchased by the death and blood of the Lamb. Voluntary death renders the Lamb (Jesus) completely worthy of our worship (Rev 5:12).

If you or someone in your group has musical abilities, you might want to stop here to sing together some of the beautiful worship songs which put these praises of Revelation to music.

Questions 5-6. See the note on question 1. Verse 14 tells us that these are the ones who have come through the "great tribulation." While this text is often understood as referring to those who have died during a seven-year period known as the "tribulation," it more likely refers to all the saints who have stayed faithful through the ages, especially those who were martyred or suffered greatly for their faith. Keep in mind that when John wrote these words, the church was under great persecution. For John, every Christian entered heaven out of the great tribulation.

The Bible assumes that Christ's followers will live as a persecuted minority (Jn 16:33; Acts 14:22; 2 Tim 3:12). Living in peace and prosperity, as many of us in the Western world do today, is quite exceptional. Living under pressure—religious, political, economic or physical—is normative, at least from the New Testament writers' perspectives.

Even today, following Jesus often involves suffering. In their book *By Their Blood,* James and Marti Hefley document the fact that more Christians have died for their faith in the twentieth century than in the previous nineteen centuries combined. This reality of suffering and tribulation can foster discussion related to ourselves ("Am I ready for persecution?") or related to the church around the world which still suffers (see Heb 13:3).

Question 7. Assuming that group members come from church traditions representing a wide variety of worship styles, expect varied answers. The key point is to notice that the Revelation-style worship is very God-focused (observe vv. 10 and 12), bowing in adoration to God's character, acknowledging his saving work and praising his attributes. The worshipers in Revelation focus more on "who God is" in contrast to some modern worship songs which emphasize more "my experience with God" or "how God makes me feel."

Question 8. Here we revisit the lessons of study eight: the vision of heaven and of this heavenly crosscultural worship service gives us grace to endure hardship.

The first Anglo crosscultural missionary from North America, Adoniram Judson, had the Revelation 7:9 worship service in mind when he wrote to his future father-in-law asking for Nancy's hand in marriage.

> I have now to ask, whether you can consent to part with your daughter early next Spring, to see her no more in this world; whether you can consent to her departure, and her subjection to the hardships and sufferings of a missionary life; whether you can consent to the dangers of the ocean; to the fatal influence of the southern climate of India; to every kind of want and distress; to degradation, insult, persecution, and perhaps even a violent death.
>
> Can you consent to all this, for the sake of him who left his heavenly throne, and died for her and for you; for the sake of the perishing, immortal souls; for the sake of Zion, and the glory of God? Can you consent to all this, in hope of soon meeting your daughter in the world of glory, with the crown of righteousness, brightened with the acclamations of praise which shall redound to her

Savior from the heathens saved, through her means, from eternal woe and despair? (Courtney Anderson, *To the Golden Shore* [Valley Forge: Judson Press, 1987], p. 83).

Every one of Judson's bleak predictions came true in Nancy's life, but the vision too was fulfilled. Today there are millions of people from several ethnic groups in Burma who point to the work of the Judsons as the key to their entrance into a relationship with Christ. They will be there in those great worship services of Revelation because the Judsons stayed faithful.

Question 9. Experts estimate that there are at least four thousand language groups with no Bible translation available and over ten thousand people groups with no vital witness for Christ. This heavenly vision of John can serve as an incentive to get people praying for people groups, adopting a country or donating to the work of pioneer evangelism around the world. Useful resources here include Patrick Johnstone's *Operation World,* as well as printed and video resources from the U.S. Center for World Missions, Wycliffe Bible Translators and the Jesus Film Project.

Question 10. Simply put, worship which includes cultural and ethnic diversity previews heaven.

Now or Later. Use this passage to show the struggles we'll all go through as the church grows outside of our own cultural comfort zones.

Paul Borthwick and his wife, Christie, serve with Development Associates International, dedicated to leadership development in the two-thirds world. In addition, Paul teaches at Gordon College in Wenham, Massachusetts. He is also the author of Six Dangerous Questions.

What Should We Study Next?

A good place to continue your study of Scripture would be with a book study. Many groups begin with a Gospel such as *Mark* (20 studies by Jim Hoover) or *John* (26 studies by Douglas Connelly). These guides are divided into two parts so that if twenty or twenty-six weeks seems like too much to do at once, the group can feel free to do half and take a break with another topic. Later you might want to come back to it. You might prefer to try a shorter letter. *Philippians* (9 studies by Donald Baker), *Ephesians* (11 studies by Andrew T. and Phyllis J. Le Peau) and *1 & 2 Timothy and Titus* (12 studies by Pete Sommer) are good options. If you want to vary your reading with an Old Testament book, consider *Ecclesiastes* (12 studies by Bill and Teresa Syrios) for a challenging and exciting study.

There are a number of interesting topical LifeGuide studies as well. Here are some options for filling three or four quarters of a year:

Basic Discipleship
Christian Beliefs, 12 studies by Stephen D. Eyre
Christian Character, 12 studies by Andrea Sterk & Peter Scazzero
Christian Disciplines, 12 studies by Andrea Sterk & Peter Scazzero
Evangelism, 12 studies by Rebecca Pippert & Ruth Siemens

Building Community
Christian Community, 12 studies by Rob Suggs
Fruit of the Spirit, 9 studies by Hazel Offner
Spiritual Gifts, 12 studies by Charles & Anne Hummel

Character Studies
New Testament Characters, 12 studies by Carolyn Nystrom
Old Testament Characters, 12 studies by Peter Scazzero
Old Testament Kings, 12 studies by Carolyn Nystrom
Women of the Old Testament, 12 studies by Gladys Hunt

The Trinity
Meeting God, 12 studies by J. I. Packer
Meeting Jesus, 13 studies by Leighton Ford
Meeting the Spirit, 12 studies by Douglas Connelly